AUTHOR-PRENEUR
BLUEPRINT

My Personal Nuggets for Becoming A Bestselling Author

DR. TENARIA DRUMMOND-SMITH

HOV
PUBLISHING

www.hovpub.com

AUTHOR-PRENEUR **BLUEPRINT**

My Personal Nuggets for Becoming A Bestselling Author

HOV Publishing is a division of HOV, LLC.
www.hovpub.com
hopeofvision@gmail.com

Front Cover Design and Inside layout by Hope of Vision Designs
Editor/Proofread: Jeff Smith

Contact the Author, Tenaria Drummond-Smith at tenariadrummondsmith@yahoo.com

For further information regarding special discounts on bulk purchases, please visit www.hovpub.com.

ISBN Paperback: 978-1-955107-78-5
ISBN Hardcase: 978-1-955107-65-5

Printed in the United States of America

DEDICATION

I dedicate this book to everyone who has a desire to become an author. I hope that my book will inspire and motivate you to begin your journey by writing your first book.

"Be the first to tell your own story. Besides, only you know the truth."

- Dr. Tenaria Drummond-Smith

AUTHOR-PRENEUR BLUEPRINT

My Personal Nuggets for Becoming A Bestselling Author

ACKNOWLEDGEMENT

I thank God for always reminding me of who He called me to be. I shall be the head, and not the tail. I can do all things through Christ that strengthens me. I thank God for choosing me to be one of His mouthpieces, for giving me boldness, and letting me know that I am more than a conqueror.

I thank God for a praying husband and business partner, my best friend Jeff Smith. I remember telling him about the vision that God gave me for this book. His response about God has always been the same. He said that if God spoke to me, then release the book. He agreed that what the Lord downloaded into me was for me to help new writers get their work published. Jeff, I thank you for understanding how important it is for me to build generational wealth behind a legacy.

I thank Germaine Miller-Summers, my publisher for the past ten years. Germaine is like family to me, and I know that when I conceptualize different book ideas, she has the patience and the capacity to bring them to life. Germaine, I thank you for always making my vision for books a reality. I really could not have done this without you, and your expertise as a publisher is valuable. I highly recommend Germaine's company, HOV Publishing, to get your books published.

And last, but not least, I thank all the Awesome Women On The Move and our supporters for helping me with this project.

TABLE OF CONTENTS

INTRODUCTION

This book was written to answer some of the many questions that I have been asked about how to become an author. I have helped over one hundred women become bestselling authors. I have shared my platform after a couple of our co-author books were advertised on Times Square billboards in New York City. This was really a big deal because people from all over the world come here to visit. Being an author has allowed me to be featured in newspapers, interviews, and speaking engagements. I give God the glory for all the great things he has done for me, especially with becoming a number one bestselling author! I am excited to share with you a little about who I am and about some of the things that helped me write my books. Everything I have done thus far has really been about me stepping out of my comfort zone to just start writing. I pray that the nuggets from my blueprint will answer some of your questions and encourage you to start writing.

I am Dr. Tenaria Drummond-Smith, the proud founder and visionary of Awesome Women On The Move ministry and movement. Since 2006, I wanted to get like-minded women together who wanted to show others how women can get together without being catty. We can get together to encourage, inspire, celebrate, and motivate each other. I wanted to make a safe space where women could share their personal stories without being judged. I wanted women to be able to be transparent when they spoke their truth. Along the way, my vision changed. Not only did I want women to feel free in speaking about their hurt and pain, but I also wanted them to feel free in writing about their trials and tribulations so that other women could be encouraged to do the same. In doing so, this ministry and movement has also become a business.

CHAPTER 1

AUTHOR-PRENEUR BLUEPRINT

When I wrote my first book, *I've Been Hurt In The Church*, it was about how life handed me some devastating blows. At times, it is the hands of those who say they know and love the Lord that will mishandle you. This book is about some of my painful experiences, but it is also about how God gave me the strength to champion through those circumstances and keep trusting that he would bring me through. Not long after this first book, I began to have visions and dreams to do books that allowed six women who had been part of the Awesome Women On The Move movement for years to share their stories along with mine. It was God's way of me showing me how to share the platform and help others get their stories out into the world. I was a new author myself, and you might be wondering how I managed to get a bunch of women together to write for one book. It was not as hard as I thought, because God gave me strategic instructions about how to get it done. Once I explained to the women what the book was about, the rest was history. I knew that everyone had a story to tell, and it was all about them being transparent in a way that readers would be able to identify with them. My goal was to help them become the first authors in their families by being free to write about things most families dare not speak about. The goal was for us to become generational curse breakers, no longer hiding in the dark and keeping hurts to ourselves. We wanted the world to know how we felt. From this, Awesome Women On The Move's first book was birthed out by God-ordained women. Our stories were purposely written to reach the saved and the unsaved women with our testimonies.

The following year, I knew I was going to do another book but was not sure what kind of book it would be. I prayed and fasted, and I heard the Lord call me an "author-preneur". I never heard that term before, so I asked the Lord about the meaning. He explained to me that an author-preneur is someone who helps others write their stories. I told my husband about what the Lord spoke to me, and he agreed that it was exactly what I was. I was not quite sure of what this second book project was going to be about, but I began having visions about helping women who wanted to become authors, but could not afford the two to three thousand dollars it might cost to publish their work. God told me that I was going to do another book that was going to be a bestseller. It was not going to be sold just on the Amazon.com platform, but it was going to see a distribution that would reach the four corners of the world. *Awesome Women On The Move: Seven Awesome Women Who Share Their Trials, Tribulations and Testimonies* was birthed out.

Now that the first co-author book was done, I felt led to do another one, and some women also asked if I was going to do another one. But this time, I wanted to be more mindful about who I was going to allow to be an author in this book. This third book was a game changer for me because instead of using authors from the first co-author book, I reached out to other women to give them a chance to write about what was in their hearts. Even though some might have written before, they never had a chance to have their work published in a book. I had a vision to do a book about love and grace, and I wanted to get women who understood the title. I knew this book would allow readers, one way or another, to identify with love in their lives. It was not difficult getting new women to participate in this book, *Awesome Women On The Move: Love Grounded By Grace*. We all thought about how God loved us to give up Jesus, his only begotten Son, to die for us. Despite us all thinking and doing things we should not, God gave us grace to repent and get things right with him. Because no two people write the same way, *Love Grounded By Grace* was a book of experiences.

My fourth book project, *The Awesome Women On The Move Inspirational Daily Journal*, came to me in a vision. The Lord told that this time around, I was going to have thirty women in this book that would become a bestseller. This came to pass. This journal was written by women from different walks of life who wrote from their hearts and shared experiences of their lives that readers could glean from. If we could put a smile on someone's face from them reading our stories, then we knew this book was not just another journal. As an encouraging collection of affirmations, scripture, and quotes, we wanted this book to have a positive impact on readers' lives. After reading the word of God, they could continue their day by reading real words from real people.

Awesome Women On The Move: Praying For Everything Under The Sun was different from all other book projects because the Lord gave me a new number: fifty. I questioned myself about whether I heard right about what God said, but then He started downloading things into my spirit that He wanted the authors to pray for. It was during the COVID-19 pandemic that the *Praying For Everything Under The Sun* came forth. Four thousand copies of this book were

<u>sold during the pre-sale campaign</u>, and this was at the beginning of the COVID-19 pandemic. If you walk in faith and set your standards high, God will do the impossible!

The Bible is clear about there being nothing new under the sun. What we experience in our lives is prophecy being fulfilled. I still believe in the power of prayer, even when it looks like God is not moving. It is my desire for everyone who reads this prophetic book to feel the power of anointed prayer. I pray that every prayer will be answered, and that people's lives will be changed. God will use answered prayers as testimonies that He still answers prayers. People will know that prayer still works. I <u>know</u> prayer works because through my answered prayer, God birthed out *Awesome Women On The Move: What It Is Like Being A Woman,* the sixth book and fifth co-author book.

JOURNAL NOTES: *"Don't just read the chapter, write notes to glean from"*
~Dr. Tenaria Drummond-Smith

JOURNAL NOTES: *"Don't just read the chapter, write notes to glean from"*

~Dr. Tenaria Drummond-Smith

JOURNAL NOTES: *"Don't just read the chapter, write notes to glean from"*
~Dr. Tenaria Drummond-Smith

CHAPTER 2

FIVE BLUEPRINT NUGGETS

Writing a book does not have to be as hard as some people make it out to be. We all have a story to tell. It just needs to be written. The point where I see most people having trouble is with getting started. Before you start to write, I suggest that you have an idea of what you want to write about. I will give you an example, and I pray that this information helps you. Keep in mind that everything in your story must flow. Also remember that every introduction is different because everything depends on what you are writing about.

Hello, my name is Kim, and I live with my grandmother in a three family house in Brooklyn, New York. My family lives on the top floor. I am feeling really excited because I started high school last week. The good thing about my new school is that I can walk there. On my first day of school, I met some new classmates. While were in class, our teacher asked that we all introduce ourselves to each other. We were also asked to exchange phone numbers just in case someone is absent from class one day. That way, we could reach out to them and get them the homework for that day.

Here are a few topics that people write about:

- What it is like losing a family member, friend, or pet
- What it is like being single
- What it is like being married
- What it was like being addicted to a person, place, or thing

Once you begin to write on your topic, everything else will begin to flow. Keep in mind that it is <u>your</u> story, and you are writing about your feelings and emotions. You are writing about how you dealt with different situations in your life –whether good, bad, or indifferent.

JOURNAL NOTES: *"Don't just read the chapter, write notes to glean from"*
~Dr. Tenaria Drummond-Smith

JOURNAL NOTES: *"Don't just read the chapter, write notes to glean from"*

~Dr. Tenaria Drummond-Smith

CHAPTER 3

THE PROS OF BEING AN AUTHOR

Even though every author receives different benefits, I am dropping nuggets about some things that applied to me. First off, it really depends on the publishing company you sign up with. I advise all inspiring authors to reach every publishing company that you feel might be interested in getting your book published. Not all publishing companies will give you the rights to your documents once they are published. The publisher I signed up with agreed to this. I have the rights to all my books, and I can use my material in other books at any given time. This arrangement has helped my books get distributed in major outlets like Target, Walmart, Amazon, Barnes & Noble, and BookBaby. Having a published book can help you to get speaking engagements and media attention. Perhaps you might want to consider turning your book into a play, a movie, or even a book series to keep your readers in suspense. Maybe you can start your own book club with other authors and exchange ideas. If you market your book well, you can make a lot of money for yourself…but it also depends on how far outside the box you are willing to go in order to sell your book!

JOURNAL NOTES: *"Don't just read the chapter, write notes to glean from"*
~Dr. Tenaria Drummond-Smith

JOURNAL NOTES: *"Don't just read the chapter, write notes to glean from"*

~Dr. Tenaria Drummond-Smith

CHAPTER 4

THE CONS OF BEING AN AUTHOR

You might think that you have written a good story for your book. The truth of the matter is that readers do not always read the same types of books. People choose books for different reasons. When someone chooses a book to buy, they are often captivated by their interest in the title and the book jacket. This is not always the case though.

If you choose to self-publish, you may run into issues from some printing companies. The text on the pages may not line up properly, or the pages might begin to come loose from a weak binding. There could be grammatical errors that show up. I mention these things to say that being an author is not some way to get rich quick, like some people might think. I am not saying that it is not possible, but it is not likely to happen that way.

Whether we all realize or not, God gives us visions and dreams. Many times, we do not act on them right away because we get distracted by what we see other people doing, or by words that are spoken to us. If you have the desire to do a thing, go forth and do it without distraction. Keep in mind that you cannot always share your dreams with others. If you are not careful, you might find out the hard way that you are having conversations with dream snatchers. They will make it seem as if your dreams are not worthwhile or that they belong to somebody else. The dream snatcher might even make it seem that your dream belonged to them <u>first</u>! Instead of encouraging you, they distract you away from what you need to concentrate on. And then there are the haters…yes, the undercover haters who have no problem looking for every flaw they can find with your vision. Everybody makes mistakes, so getting some constructive criticism is welcome. However, the criticism might not be constructive when your mistakes are the <u>only</u> thing they ever communicate to you –regardless of any success that you have. Haters and dream snatchers might offer you opinions about what they think you should do, even though they have no experience with where you are trying to go. They are a distraction. Chase after your vision without distraction and surround yourself with people who want to see you succeed.

I always tell people that I will show them better than I can tell them.

USING MY FIVE BLUEPRINT NUGGETS TO GET STARTED

1. Who are you? Readers are always interested in knowing who the writer is.

2. What inspired you? Readers like to know about the foundation of your story.

3. Why did you choose this time to present your story? Readers like to know why you presented your book when you did. Was it a quick work? Or did the project take a long time?

4. How did you find your publisher? Readers might want to know how you did your research.

5. When did you find the time to write? Many times, authors write a little material at a time because it helps them avoid writer's block.

Keep in mind that someone could invite you to tell your story in a location that may require you to travel. They might love your style of writing and appreciate the positive impact that it is making on lives. Are you willing to do this? When you are invited to someone's event, be sure to ask if there will be other authors selling books as well. This way, you can determine if it would be a good idea for you to sell at the same event, especially if you are all selling the same type of books.

JOURNAL NOTES: *"Don't just read the chapter, write notes to glean from"*
~Dr. Tenaria Drummond-Smith

JOURNAL NOTES: *"Don't just read the chapter, write notes to glean from"*

~Dr. Tenaria Drummond-Smith

CHAPTER 5

WHY HAVING A BOOK SIGNING IS IMPORTANT

I believe every author should always do a book signing. This will allow your readers to meet you in person, to be able to get to know you, and to have photos taken with you. It also allows readers to receive a signed copy of the book they purchased. You will be able to see a slice of what your target audience looks like. You will be able to identify them by age, gender, and ethnic groups. This type of setting will give your readers a chance to speak with you and ask questions about your book or any other projects you might have coming up. You should always be on the lookout for events where you can place yourself along with other authors.

PLACES TO CONSIDER HAVING A BOOK SIGNING

1. There are some community centers where you can rent space to give yourself a book signing. I like them because they allow people to see what others around them are doing. This is an exchange network for people in your neighborhood.

2. The libraries would be great to host a book signing because people are always there picking up and returning books. This is the place for readers. For another idea, you can do a reading of one your book chapters. This will help to get your story out there.

3. School events sometimes host a "career day" to encourage current students and show them what former students have achieved. You can be one of those achievers.

4. Barnes & Noble is an excellent place for a book signing because they like to showcase new authors.

5. Restaurants are another place to host book signings. You might guess that you have to spend some money on food, and you might be right. We know that everything comes with a price.

6. Street fairs are very good because of the foot traffic.

7. Some churches might host book signings for their members.

8. Selling your books from your vehicle. I have never done it before, but it is an idea.

9. Book fairs are good to attend because you are able to meet other authors while trying to sell your own books. Many times, authors do book swaps with each other.

10. Coffee shops are another place where you could host a book signing.

11. Family reunions are very popular because they give you a chance to show your family members what you have been doing.

12. Although you are a new author, you might want to consider having your own workshop where you can sell your book.

13. Conferences are good places to consider, regardless of you not being the one hosting them. You will be able to meet people from all walks of life.

JOURNAL NOTES: *"Don't just read the chapter, write notes to glean from"*

~Dr. Tenaria Drummond-Smith

JOURNAL NOTES: *"Don't just read the chapter, write notes to glean from"*
~Dr. Tenaria Drummond-Smith

JOURNAL NOTES: *"Don't just read the chapter, write notes to glean from"*

~Dr. Tenaria Drummond-Smith

CHAPTER 6

CHOOSING A PUBLISHING COMPANY THAT IS RIGHT FOR YOU

There are thousands of publishing companies around the world, but not all publishing contracts are the same. My suggestion is to do thorough research on any publishing company you might have your eye on. Recommendations from other authors can sometimes help with choosing a publisher. Make sure the publishing company is listed under the Better Business Bureau and has positive reviews. These are some things you should have in mind to ask:

1. Do I have any say in designing my book cover?
2. Do I have to edit my work?
3. Will I need someone to proofread my manuscript?
4. Do I have all rights to my book?
5. How many copies of my book will I receive?
6. Who gets the pre-sale money from my book?

7. Can I use my own printing company once the book is published? Or do I have to buy them only from the publishing company?

WHAT SHOULD BE LISTED IN YOUR CONTRACT

Before signing a contract, have the publisher give you clarity on any uncertainties. Remember that a contract is a <u>legal </u>document.

1. Professionally formatted interior layout
2. Copyright
3. ISBNs with barcode for retail availability
4. Library of Congress control number (LCCN)
5. Worldwide distribution (Amazon, Barnes and Noble, etc.)

JOURNAL NOTES: *"Don't just read the chapter, write notes to glean from"*
~Dr. Tenaria Drummond-Smith

JOURNAL NOTES: *"Don't just read the chapter, write notes to glean from"*

~Dr. Tenaria Drummond-Smith

CHAPTER 7

WHY YOU SHOULD CONSIDER PRODUCING A CO-AUTHOR BOOK

What is the meaning of a co-author? A co-author is an author who works with one or more different authors to write something. If three authors contribute their chapters along with yours in one book, each person calls themselves a co-author. You might be under another author's book project, but no doubt –you are still an author.

My personal experience of doing co-author book projects has been challenging at times, but is has been good. I had to deal with multiple personalities. I often found myself interviewing women for my books because I needed to see if some who said they were ready to share their stories were really willing to do it. For some, the release was harder than they thought, but others found ways to identify with what they felt and pushed through their pain to write. Before moving forward with the book, all co-authors were made to understand the vision that I had. My goal has always been to motivate an author to write more than what is required because it helps their writing flow. One chapter is what they were asked for, but the overflow could turn into their own book. All they had to do was to keep writing in the flow.

Sometimes while managing a co-author project, you will begin to see some weak links. Why? Because not all authors write with the same confidence. There might be authors who start out doing well, but then fear comes to their mind and they begin thinking their story is not good enough. If you ever begin to feel this way, my suggestion to you is to stop writing. Take a break so you can gather your thoughts and write with clarity.

Many times, I have been told by co-authors that they were brought to tears when they began writing about themselves. I believe in writing as a form of release from hurt and pain. It really has become a form of therapy that allows our stories to be shared with the world. However, as a published author, you will be careful about what you want people to know and what you want to keep to yourself. There are some things that you will take with you to your grave –just keeping it real.

When I have one-on-one conversations with potential co-authors, I will already have a list of topics that they could write about because they most likely have never written for a book before. I also have them choose a topic so I can give them tips on how to get their writing started. Let us be clear: when you write, you do not always have to begin by writing about yourself. It all depends on the kind of story you have to tell, and how you want to pull your readers into your story. The more you write, the more you will learn about how to captivate your audience.

WHY YOU SHOULD HAVE YOUR WORK PROOFREAD

Proofreading is so, so necessary! No one wants to purchase a book that has a lot of errors in the manuscript. Another set of eyes are always good for reviewing, even if your work is being edited by your publisher. Never allow the editor to change your context of your story, especially when they use words that are not a part of your current vocabulary. Never be afraid to tell the editor that you disagree with any changes they want to make in your work. You might use some slang words that they may not think suitable for what you have written.

Keep in mind that your story is <u>your</u> story, and <u>you do have an audience that will</u> <u>be able to relate to your style of writing</u>. Make sure your story reads well to grab your readers' attention.

WHY YOU SHOULD ALWAYS SET A DEADLINE FOR COMPLETING YOUR BOOK

When you do a book project with two or more authors, do yourself a favor by having a date in mind to complete the project and have the book released. If you do not create a deadline, the book will never be completed. You should keep emphasizing to yourself and your co-authors that when the chapters are submitted—sooner rather than later—for editing and corrections, the publisher can forward the final manuscript for printing. Once that part is done, the focus can now go towards the book pre-sale.

JOURNAL NOTES: *"Don't just read the chapter, write notes to glean from"*

~Dr. Tenaria Drummond-Smith

JOURNAL NOTES: *"Don't just read the chapter, write notes to glean from"*
~Dr. Tenaria Drummond-Smith

CHAPTER 8

WHAT IS A BOOK PRE-SALE

A pre-sale involves getting people to order your book before it is available to purchase directly from you or through the distributor, i.e., Amazon, Barnes and Noble, etc. The good thing about doing a pre-sale is that you can have it for as long as you might need to, but please keep mind that some of your customers might get tired of waiting to receive their book. Pre-sales are good, but you do not want to turn away your customers. After all, nobody wants to wait *that* long for something they paid for. I suggest doing a pre-sale that should last anywhere from thirty to no more than sixty days. This way, you can keep people excited about your new book release.

HOW TO GET YOUR PRE-SALE GOING

1. Take the time to write down a list of family members and friends so you can contact them about the pre-sale. Have

everyone in your book project do the same. With all co-authors working together, this will help boost your book sale numbers.

2. Get a list of emails addresses for everyone you know. I suggest this would now be a good time to use those business cards you collected over the years. Email them about your new book release.

3. Use all your social media platforms: Facebook, Twitter, Instagram, Pinterest, LinkedIn, etc.

4. Have flyers and a postcard designed that advertise your book.

I tried different ways of increasing sales for my book. Not everything worked, but I never gave up on myself. I believed that if success was happening for other authors, it would surely happen for me. The good thing about it is that I did not have to pay someone two or three-thousand dollars to make it happen. What I did notice was that if I sold at least a hundred copies of my book, my chances of becoming a bestseller were greater than if I had just sold a few books.

CHECKING YOUR AMAZON SELLER STATUS

Once you choose categories for your books, Amazon starts tallying where your books are sold. If you market yourself well, you can become a bestselling author on Amazon in five minutes. The key is to keep checking Amazon's sale count because the numbers change during the day. By Amazon's standard, a one to one-hundred ranking on their list makes you a bestseller. When you see an orange banner placed over your book image, you have made number one status! The thing about being an Amazon bestseller is that you could have a number five ranking at one moment, and then you could be at a number fifty-five ranking in less than thirty minutes. Another thing to keep in mind is that your other selected categories could give you a number one ranking.

HOW TO BECOME A NEW YORK TIMES BESTSELLER

Achieving a New York Times bestselling book status is much harder than Amazon. Not only do you have to sell at least five-thousand copies within one week, but they also have to be diverse sales, meaning that you cannot sell five-thousand books to a pre-existing list of followers through a personal website that you might sell on. But all things are possible if you have a plan. It is truly my desire to become a New York Times bestseller!

JOURNAL NOTES: *"Don't just read the chapter, write notes to glean from"*
~Dr. Tenaria Drummond-Smith

JOURNAL NOTES: *"Don't just read the chapter, write notes to glean from"*
~Dr. Tenaria Drummond-Smith

CHAPTER 9

WRITE THE VISION AND MAKE IT PLAIN

The purpose of me writing this short book was to take time and share some things I learned along the way to becoming an author. I had to learn on my own because I had no one who could take time to teach me. Some of my book project co-authors brought to my attention that they knew authors, but when they asked them for help in getting started, no one responded. When I started encouraging them, it was not a big deal for me to share with them what I learned. Along the way, I understood that some people out there want the glory all for themselves. Anyone who has ever been in an Awesome Women On The Move co-author book project knows that I allowed them to participate in more than one project. It has been my goal to birth out authors so they would become bestselling authors. I believe that one day, our books will be turned into plays, short films, and movies. I pray this book answered your questions and inspired you. Write your vision and make it plain.

THIS IS WHO I AM

These affirmations and Bible verses are for every young and not-so-young person to read and speak over yourselves to be encouraged. Whether you had a bad day, have a hard time dealing with someone, feel like you want to give up, or feel like you do not fit in, there is something here for you. I pray these words will begin to help you see yourselves differently and walk in the beauty of who God created you to be.

REMEMBER TO SAY THAT "I AM!"

I AM THE HEAD, AND NOT THE TAIL. I WILL ALWAYS HAVE MONEY IF I WORK FOR IT AND SAVE IT.

"*And the Lord shall make thee the head, and not the tail; and thou shalt be above only, and thou shalt not be beneath; if that thou hearken unto the commandments of the Lord thy God, which I command thee this day, to observe and to do them:*"

Deuteronomy 28:13

I AM FEARFULLY AND WONDERFULLY MADE. I LOVE EVERYTHING ABOUT MYSELF.

"I will praise thee; for I am fearfully and wonderfully made: marvellous are thy works; and that my soul knoweth right well."

Psalm 139:14

WHEN I STAY FOCUSED, I AM ABLE TO DO ANYTHING I SET MY MIND TO DO. I HAVE BIG DREAMS FOR MY FUTURE. I WILL ALWAYS TELL MYSELF THAT I CAN DO ALL THINGS.

"I can do all things through Christ which strengtheneth me."

Philippians 4:13

I AM WILLING TO STUDY HARD TO GET GOOD GRADES. IT IS MY DESIRE TO BREAK MY FAMILY'S GENERATION CURSES.

"And it shall come to pass in that day, that his burden shall be taken away from off thy shoulder, and his yoke from off thy neck, and the yoke shall be destroyed because of the anointing."

Isaiah 10:27

I AM ABLE TO START MY OWN BUSINESS SOMEDAY, OR EVEN BECOME AN AUTHOR TO INSPIRE OTHERS. WE ALL HAVE A STORY TO TELL.

"...Write the vision, and make it plain upon tables, that he may run that readeth it."

Habakkuk 2:2

IT DOES NOT MATTER WHETHER I AM A MAN OR WOMAN. WE ARE ALL HERE TO BRING CHANGE TO THE WORLD.

"And unto one he gave five talents, to another two, and to another one; to every man according to his several ability..."

Matthew 25:15

I AM ABLE TO FORGIVE, EVEN AFTER I HAVE BEEN MISTREATED. FORGIVENESS ALLOWS ME TO RELEASE THINGS BOTTLED UP INSIDE AND HELPS ME TO TELL MY STORY UNAPOLOGETICALLY.

"And be ye kind one to another, tenderhearted, forgiving one another, even as God for Christ's sake hath forgiven you."

Ephesians 4:32

I WILL BE RESPECTFUL TO MY PARENTS, TEACHERS, AND AUTHORITY FIGURES. THEY ARE HERE TO GUIDE AND INSTRUCT US TOWARD THE RIGHT THINGS.

"Honour thy father and mother; which is the first commandment with promise; that it may be well with thee, and thou mayest live long on the earth."

Ephesians 6:2-3

"Submit yourselves to every ordinance of man for the Lord's sake: whether it be to the king, as supreme; or unto governors, as unto them that are sent by him for the punishment of evildoers, and for the praise of them that do well."

1 Peter 2:13-14

I AM ABLE TO VOICE MY OPINION WHEN NECESSARY. WE ALL HAVE THE RIGHT TO DO SO, BUT WE MUST BE MINDFUL THAT WORDS CAN HURT A PERSON'S FEELING. NO ONE SHOULD EVER WANT TO OFFEND ANOTHER PERSON INTENTIONALLY.

"Even so the tongue is a little member, and boasteth great things. Behold, how great a matter a little fire kindleth! And the tongue is a fire, a world of iniquity: so is the tongue among our members, that it defileth the whole body, and setteth on fire the course of nature; and it is set on fire of hell. For every kind of beasts, and of birds, and of serpents, and of things in the sea, is tamed, and hath been tamed of mankind: but the tongue can no man tame; it is an unruly evil, full of deadly poison."

James 3:5-8

I AM NOT AFRAID TO APOLOGIZE TO SOMEONE I OFFENDED. I CAN GO TO THE PERSON AND TRY TO MAKE THINGS RIGHT IF I HURT THEM.

"Therefore if thou bring thy gift to the altar, and there rememberest that thy brother hath ought against thee; leave there thy gift before the altar, and go thy way; first be reconciled to thy brother, and then come and offer thy gift."

Matthew 5:23-24

I AM NOT ASHAMED OF THE GOSPEL, BUT EVERYONE IS ENTITLED TO THEIR BELIEFS. AS FOR ME, I WILL ALWAYS GIVE THANKS UNTO THE LORD BECAUSE HE IS WORTHY OF MY PRAISE. IF IT WAS NOT FOR GOD, I TRULY DO NOT KNOW WHERE I WOULD BE. I THANK GOD EVERYDAY!

"For I am not ashamed of the gospel of Christ: for it is the power of God unto salvation to every one that believeth; to the Jew first, and also to the Greek. For therein is the righteousness of God revealed from faith to faith: as it is written, The just shall live by faith."

Romans 1:16-17

"Let every thing that hath breath praise the LORD. Praise ye the LORD."

Psalm 150:6

IF I SEE SOMEONE WHO LOOKS LIKE THEY ARE IN NEED, I MAKE IT MY JOB TO PRAY FOR THEM. IF I CAN, I TRY TO HELP THEM. I WOULD WANT SOMEONE ELSE TO DO THE SAME FOR ME.

"But a certain Samaritan, as he journeyed, came where he was: and when he saw him, he had compassion on him, and went to him, and bound up his wounds, pouring in oil and wine, and set him on his own beast, and brought him to an inn, and took care of him."

Luke 10:33-34

I AM NOT AFRAID TO ASK FOR HELP. WE ALL NEED HELP SOMETIMES. IF I DO NOT ASK FOR HELP WHEN I NEED IT, I CANNOT EXPECT OTHERS TO READ MY MIND.

"And, behold, two blind men sitting by the way side, when they heard that Jesus passed by, cried out, saying, Have mercy on us, O Lord, thou son of David."

Matthew 20:30

I AM AN INSPIRING AUTHOR WAITING TO TELL MY STORY. I BELIEVE THERE IS A STORY IN ALL OF US. WE HAVE TO BE WILLING TO SHARE IT TO HELP OTHERS.

"That which we have seen and heard declare we unto you, that ye also may have fellowship with us…"

1 John 1:3

I AM A GENERATION CURSE BREAKER. MY FAMILY MAY NOT OWN MUCH, BUT I WANT TO BE THE FIRST ONE IN MY FAMILY TO CHANGE THAT. I WILL REMIND MYSELF THAT ALL THINGS ARE POSSIBLE.

"And Jesus looking upon them saith, With men it is impossible, but not with God: for with God all things are possible."

Mark 10:27

I AM SOMEONE WHO STARTS AND ENDS MY DAY IN PRAYER. WHEN I PRAY, I HAVE THE HOPE THAT EVERYTHING IS GOING TO BE ALRIGHT, EVEN WHEN I DO NOT UNDERSTAND EVERYTHING.

"O God, thou art my God; early will I seek thee: my soul thirsteth for thee, my flesh longeth for thee in a dry and thirsty land, where no water is;"

Psalm 63:1

I WILL LOVE EVERYONE. I WILL LOVE SOMEONE EVEN WHEN THEY DO NOT WANT TO BE LOVED. I WILL SHOW LOVE EVERYWHERE I GO.

"A new commandment I give unto you, That ye love one another; as I have loved you, that ye also love one another."

John 13:34

I AM GRATEFUL TO HAVE FOOD, WATER, CLOTHING, AND A PLACE TO LAY MY HEAD. I ALWAYS WANT TO BE GRATEFUL FOR WHAT I HAVE AND NOT TAKE THINGS FOR GRANTED. I WILL NOT COMPLAIN BECAUSE I KNOW THAT BY FAITH, THINGS WILL CHANGE FOR THE BETTER. I WILL KEEP THE FAITH!

"I know both how to be abased, and I know how to abound: every where and in all things I am instructed both to be full and to be hungry, both to abound and to suffer need."

Philippians 4:12

AUTHOR'S DECLARATION TO SELF
(meaning YOU!)

"Now faith is the substance of things hoped for, the evidence of things not seen…but without faith it is impossible to please him: for he that cometh to God must believe that he is, and that he is a rewarder of them that diligently seek him."

Hebrews 11:1,6

I HAVE A STORY TO TELL. I WILL NO LONGER BE AFRAID TO WRITE ABOUT THINGS THAT HAPPENED IN MY LIFE, WHETHER GOOD OR BAD. I NO LONGER HAVE TO QUESTION MYSELF ABOUT HOW I WILL BEGIN TO WRITE. I WILL USE THE NUGGETS FROM THIS BOOK TO GET STARTED. I WILL TRY TO WRITE EVERY DAY. IF I STAY CONSISTENT, I WILL SEE THE RESULT OF MY FIRST COMPLETED BOOK. I DO NOT WANT TO JUST BE AN AUTHOR. I WANT TO BE A BESTSELLING AUTHOR.

I AM WRITING AND SPEAKING THIS INTO EXISTENCE.

SIGN_____

DATE_____

A MESSAGE TO THE READER

I am always looking for new co-authors to participate in Awesome Women On The Move book projects. We collaborate with women from nation to nation, and from state to state. You do not have to know me to become a part of this movement. The Awesome Women On The Move ministry and movement began locally, but it is becoming a global force.

I coach new authors. If you need help in getting started, I can help (see details on the rear cover).

I look forward to speaking with and meeting you!

"NO MORE DELAYS"

ABOUT THE AUTHOR

Dr. Tenaria Drummond-Smith, an ambitious and multi-talented entrepreneur, is the founder and visionary of Awesome Women On The Move, Inc., a 501(c)(3) company. As a native New Yorker and former civil service employee, she was motivated to reinvent herself after experiencing a series of impactful life changes. Her personal ministry was birthed in 2006 and it has blossomed into a movement and an organization that promotes fellowship and unity among all women by the love of God through Jesus Christ.

Dr. Tenaria has the God-given vision and heart to celebrate women who do phenomenal things but are rarely recognized. Her self-defined purpose is to serve as a platform to showcase women who have impacted the lives of others around them. Awesome Women On The Move has an established Facebook. com presence of 900,000+ followers (in conjunction with the Awesome Women On The Move Blog, also on Facebook), while Tenaria has a growing social media presence as a one-woman influencer through Instagram, LinkedIn, and YouTube.

The breakthrough publishing of Dr. Tenaria's first book, *I've Been Hurt In The Church*, jumpstarted her expanding list of personal and professional achievements. Following this first release of five Awesome Women On The Move featured books co-authored with women who were willing to share their stories of pain, inspiration, and encouragement:

Over 100 Awesome Women who shared their stories of Trials, Tribulations and Testimonies in...

- *Awesome Women On The Move*
- *Love Grounded By Grace*
- *Inspirational Daily Journal* (**Amazon Bestseller**)
- *National Prayer Book: Praying For Everything Under The Sun* (**#1 Amazon Bestseller**)
- *What It Is Like Being A Woman* (**Amazon Bestseller**)

AWOTM BOOKS

Dr. Tenaria received inspiration from a visit to the National Museum of African American History and Culture (NMAAHC) in Washington, D.C. She saw an exhibit of an original shawl worn by Harriet Tubman in 1911, and was deeply impacted by it. She prayed about designing her own line of shawls, and without using any patterns, the SWAG SHAWL was born. A specially-created SWAG SHAWL design is now being featured at the Harriet Tubman Museum and Educational Center in Cambridge, Maryland. For more details and/or press inquiries, Dr. Tenaria may be contacted by phone at (917) 603-8647 or by email at tenariadrummondsmith@gmail.com.

With various completed and pending projects on her plate, Dr. Tenaria Drummond-Smith is a trailblazer and a dynamic industry embodied in one woman. With her vision, there is always more to come.

"YOU HAVE A STORY TO TELL"

"WRITE YOUR STORY"

JOURNAL NOTES:

JOURNAL NOTES:

JOURNAL NOTES:

JOURNAL NOTES:

JOURNAL NOTES:

_____

_____

_____

_____

_____

_____

_____

_____

_____

_____

_____

_____

_____

_____

_____

JOURNAL NOTES:

_____

_____

_____

_____

_____

_____

_____

_____

_____

_____

_____

_____

_____

_____

JOURNAL NOTES:

JOURNAL NOTES:

JOURNAL NOTES:

JOURNAL NOTES:

JOURNAL NOTES:

JOURNAL NOTES:

JOURNAL NOTES:

JOURNAL NOTES:

JOURNAL NOTES:

JOURNAL NOTES:

JOURNAL NOTES:

JOURNAL NOTES:

CPSIA information can be obtained
at www.ICGtesting.com
Printed in the USA
BVHW021905220623
666251BV00004B/323

9 781955 107655